REDSTREAKS

A BOOK OF POEMS

PAUL BINDING

Shoestring Press

Printed by imprintdigital
Upton Pyne, Exeter
www.digital.imprint.co.uk

Typesetting and cover design by narrator
www.narrator.me.uk
info@narrator.me.uk
033 022 300 39

Published by Shoestring Press
19 Devonshire Avenue, Beeston, Nottingham, NG9 1BS
(0115) 925 1827
www.shoestringpress.co.uk

First published 2020
© Copyright: Paul Binding

The moral right of the author has been asserted.

ISBN 978-1-912524-45-7

i.m. Harvey
my incomparable collie and companion
on all the expeditions that gave rise
to these poems

CONTENTS

'Deep in the Heart of Texas'   1

Benchmarker   4

Theatre of the Absurd   6

Andy   10

'Vast Scratch-Armies'   13

In Archenfield   14

Redstreaks   18

Envoy   21

'DEEP IN THE HEART OF TEXAS'

'Deep in the Heart of Texas'—that's what the
band—'group' 'd be anachronistic—was playing
in our refurbished Village Hall as, fed up to the
back teeth, I pushed open side-door and stepped
out of sweat and din into a New Year's Eve
revelry-free. And there (but I'd guessed) you were,
leaning in wait for me against the
newly creosoted wall, pissed leer on face.
I should have said, 'Don't look at me like that,
Garth, we spent all damn' summer building
you a canoe—and at apple-harvesting
you and me raced the Harbison lot—and won.'
But as ever I waited for first words from *you*!

They were: 'Not dancing with you? Why would she
want to, after knowing *me*? You couldn't
expect someone as special as Ryllie to
so much as *look* at you, let alone *like* you:
Howard Davies, our local auctioneer's son.
No chance for *him* against her brother right
beside you in this car-park getting his balls
frozen off. Talking of which, you do understand,
Howard, how he alone satisfies her, don't you?
Garth and Amaryllis, our choice names
are badges of deep distinction. To us
other people's rules simply don't apply.'

Ghastly the instant headlines in my tabloid
brain! I must ignore them. I turned away,
tugged back open the Hall's side-door, and eyed
again the crowded merrymaking I'd just quit:
'The stars at *night*,/are big and *bright*' (clap-clap-clap-clap)
'Deep in the Heart of Texas'. And Ryllie was dancing,
silver shoes, flame-red dress and dark pony-tail
bouncing on her back. Hard to tell her partner
in all the black-tied, cummerbunded throng,

1

but not me, and—not her brother Garth.
'Reminds me *of* the one I *love*' (clap-clap-clap-clap)
'Deep in the Heart of Texas.'
                                    The night here was starless,
clouds bulging downward with forecast snow.
Banging the side-door shut, I met Garth's still broad
leer with eyes of defiance, yet he asked me:
'Shall I kiss it better, Howard?'
                          Even these last years
my fists've sent him flying across car-park
with hopes of him falling hard and bloody.
But all I managed was: 'You want to watch
your mouth, Garth, and take a look inside that
swollen head of yours. Wouldn't be a pretty sight.'

As I spoke, I thought for sure I'd done with you
and your 'special' sister, done with you both
for as much 'ever' as if I'd really fisted you into void.
'Deep in the Heart of Texas'—yes, the band was still
pounding that out, dancers giving their idiot claps….

You all must know how beyond our Village Hall great
cider orchards stretch. Some'd one day be Garth's,
some the Harbison boys'—but all of 'em might come
under my dad's hammer, indeed some already had.
With the Wye's impatient winter surge on my right,
I now ran and ran, in hired dress suit, through
the avenues of nude cider trees, though even at
this hour, in this season, I knew their identities:
Foxwhelp, Redstreak, Red Splash, Handsome Hereford,
super names, super fruit, super drink,
and one day I'd come back here—using
my dad's hammer to save or restore them.
'The stars at night/are big and bright/Deep in
the Heart of Texas.' Hot and wild out there
no doubt but no snobs bragging their incest
to summertime pals judged low in social standing.
It'd be a long road over, with gunfights and jails

2

to deal with. Still I'd chance it (clap-clap-clap-clap).
At harvesting wasn't I the expert picker of all?

Not even then had I realised how long the straight
lines of trees were (Green Wilding now, Kingston Black).
Remorseless miles they made up that night; no wonder
my patent leather shoes got filled with cold water.

Likely no revels in our Village Hall this coming
New Year, our whole land stilled and unsociable
with virus, while that great heart of Texas
beats despondent, its death toll rising hugely,
the old Rio Grande banked by heartbreak.
Ryllie (my ex) and our easy-going son
both marooned in London, somewhere I've
never felt at home.... I think of Dad, and how,
in grim turn-about, the hammer came down on
his own body, that fatal stroke at auction-time.
Garth, in case you didn't know, got returned
to Westminster last December. At *his* age!
I can't feel pleased, but may he not be the one
who'll save the apples our Herefordshire Pomona
lists so lovingly: Foxwhelp, Redstreak, Kingston Black?
They're all ripening now, whatever the rainstorms
thrashing the trees, waiting for pickers.

BENCHMARKER

'Oh, Ivo Harbison, he'll never come to anything!'
they'd say—and what a large number made up
that 'they'—parents, relations, teachers, neighbours.
Sometimes I'd turn humorous. '"Anything"
implies having no limits as to shape or size.
So couldn't it be that I'll chance upon "anything"
without me—or other people—realising?'
'Typical Ivo!' they'd shrug, 'make a serious
point, and he will joke and smile it away!'

But I was (am) very serious. I lost that
picking contest against Garth and his mate
'cos I didn't care twopence, as we'd put it then,
which side won, and rivals' banter was boring.
I lost my job in the family firm—or rather
it lost me, was redefined as a post
'not for someone with *your* priorities.'
I lost my marriage before it even began
and my lovely daughter before she could speak.
Yes, there's been a relationship or two since,
plus a step-child who liked me for a while
as I liked her or him, but all that dissolved—
as brilliant reds and golds of September will;
the crimson berries on mountain ash can't last
but I can smile at them while they're with us
as I've smiled my way through jobs at Town Halls.
'He always made us feel cheerful,' folk said
at my leaving do's, the same who'd whispered
'You know he's connected with *the* Harbisons,
don't you? But land and property aren't his line!'
And of course I've done my (little) bit for this
or that, standing somewhere, walking somewhere else,
but for what I've usually forgotten by end of week!

You could say my main contribution to life
now is smiling, as I sit, for hours on end
on this bench by the Red Lion, Bredwardine
(where else?), as neatly turned out as I can be,
shaving most days, hair-cut every five weeks
over in Leominster, regular change of sweater,
and Army Surplus trousers (survival kit).
I smile at people I grew up alongside,
some of 'em so changed by the years they don't
know who I am, at the folk in the vicinity
now proudly living in cottages I recall
the mean squash and stink of, and at all those
who've set themselves up in eco-houses
in dialogue with sunlight itself.
Perhaps I smile less at members of the 'vast
scratch-armies' of male young, but even there
you find visitors with admiring gaze
who make reverent ways to our churchyard,
where lies that vicar who died here in 1879.

On a September day like this one he
noted: 'The smell of the apples very strong.
Beyond the orchards, the lone aspen was
rustling, loud and mournfully, a lament
for the departure of summer.' Even so he
honoured the '*holy* autumn day', with
the 'robin singing in the acacia', and
'a squirrel leaping in the boughs above.'

I never sought Francis Kilvert out; he was 'place'
not print. At most I read a book a month,
by choice hard-boiled American stuff I can
pick up in Leominster or, of course, in Hay.
But Kilvert wrote one sentence I don't like:
'Of all noxious animals... the most noxious
is a tourist.' Wrong! We should bless tourists,
they mean where they go to well, and so
deserve the smiles I unceasingly give them.

THEATRE OF THE ABSURD

'That was the Fifties for us,' he pronounces
at what he (not wrongly) calls their Old Folks'
Book-Club. 'Every week we'd meet'—in an empty
classroom of a local primary, with big dreary
pictures on walls, 'My Town', 'My Home', 'My Pets'—
'to discuss what Great Theatre meant, and we knew
(though all praise to our own Royal Court!)
that where it emanated from was *Paris*.
Why, Andy Gibson and I hitched to that centre of things
and actually saw the Théâtre de Poche and the
Théâtre des Noctambules.'—named for themselves,
they'd thought, stumbling across sweet flesh as tradition
decreed on those spring evening boulevards—
'And here's the Parisian wisdom we tried to impart:
that a curtain, an impassable wall
stands between us and the world, us and ourselves;
matter filling every corner, taking up all the space,
and its weight annihilating all freedom!'

True for me now in my amiable, chatty,
over-educated dotage? Time to open
another bottle of Chilean Merlot, price £5.79
at the local Co-op, and not so bad after all!

'We all aspired to write plays, the kind we could
send to the Royal Court for consideration.
For us too dead bodies would show "geometric
progression" crowding out an apartment's
human occupants; for us also rows of chairs'd
fill up with folk you could neither hear nor see!

'Alarmed by what we all concocted together,
I sometimes, to my annoyance, felt relief
when I arrived back at Edwardian blue-stuccoed
Hayfield in King's Road, and saw my two brothers,
Oliver and Thomas, at cricket practice in those nets

our father had set up on our well-trimmed front lawn.
Ol'd break off to listen to anything I chose to say;
Thomas, lauded young spin-bowler, would not.'
His relief he never confessed to Andy Gibson,
both theatre-buff and cricketer, but no home-bird,
not one of three dark-haired siblings at play,
sons of a man proud at last to be a Town Councillor.

'And did you write an Absurdist drama, Chris?'
asks a Book-Club member for whom he's poured
a half-glass of Merlot. 'No, I decided not to!'
And he spoke the truth.

                  'We had an appointed
overseer. A PhD. He came to us
on his Harley Davidson, friendly in his studied
unfriendliness (or the other way round,
depending on your—and his—mood), Ionesco,
Genet, Adamov, Beckett his mates and sparring-
partners, and he peppered his conversation—
always polemical—with 'i e' and 'e g'
and 'etceterA, etceterA, etceterA'—
and soon we did likewise. "Time, Christopher,
you exchanged dream for action, i e wrote a play."
"When time feels right, Gordon, e g this evening!"
"And when you get down to it—i e are plonked
before pen and paper, don't ever you forget
what is light grows heavy, that the transparent
turns dense, and the world oppresses—etceterA,
etceterA, etceterA!" "I shan't," I promised.

'The gables and bay windows and blue stucco
of *Hayfield* were in sight that early summer
afternoon of Sweet Williams and lilac, when
I saw him, funny old man (or oldish man), who'd
been pottering up and down King's Road all
week. He stopped, said to me, "Son of Albert Wilkins,
our latest Councillor? Of *King* Alfred should I say?"

His laughter scratched my face. "Let me tell you
about *King* Alfred, as you're his heir, how he don't
deserve to be anyone's hero. 'Cos he's a national
bloody disgrace, he is! You just think of that poor
couple with scarcely two sticks to rub together,
(unlike some who live in a house called *Hayfield*!),
man working his bum off down in the marshes,
woman making do with what scraps they'd got so
they'd have *something* inside their bellies to keep
on going. Then his *kingship* calls on their hut—disguised
as a pauper (and that's another laugh too!)—and
out of the goodness of her heart woman says yes, she'll
feed him and gladly, but could he mind the cakes
on the hearth while she went out and milked the cow?
Simple request. But could he oblige? Not His Kingship!
Not his bloody Kingship in his great importance.
Those precious cakes got burned to cinders 'cos
he was grandly dreaming of what'd bring him fame.
And so that poor old couple had no bite to eat till
the next day—their hard work, their good intentions
come to naught. D'you like *that,* King Alfred's heir?"

'Watching him tell his tale, I knew I was staring
into the very eyes of madness. There everything
surrendered to one object for hate: a corpse
was swelling beyond its bounds. At last a subject
for my Absurdist Drama? Maybe, but I wouldn't
wish to touch it with a barge-pole. It'd be
—well, sacrilege could be the right word. In fact
I wouldn't write any play at all. I'd keep going to
the Theatre group—I had friends there, Nicola,
for instance, though really I liked her non-member
sister even better, Sally. And her I married!'

The guests gone, the clearing up done, and Sally
rereading *The Ages of Gaia* for *her* book-group,
he strolls onto the hillside above their little eco-

village, realising it's just such an evening now
as he's been describing. Still light! The half-moon
has little work to do, and yet picks out brightly
some solar panels on these timber-framed
structures' roofs. The lilacs are proudest
purples as they hold themselves above the herb-
gardens. Lavender, thymes of many sorts,
and tarragon all waft scents towards him. If he
doesn't always listen to details of eco-design,
these plants—with their grey cat, Stealth, creeping
through them—give him a solace that, inexplicably ,
he feels will survive his bodily being,
just as chairs in Paris once filled up with the unseen
and unheard. Just as heroic King Alfred
burnt cakes and gave them to posterity.

ANDY

Andy out of them all not only finished
a play but had it performed, one night only,
in, of all places, the Methodists' Hall:
Mail-man, Male-man, 'anti-hero' a postman
who delivered sexy letters to every house
in a suburban close, each proposition
taken up for the audience to hoot and cheer at!
'Well, that's the first of my many triumphs!'
Andy grinned. Christopher thought it
an appropriate start: Andy himself was sexy.

Those were the great jeans years when you could make
your crutch conspicuous if you walked in a
certain way, in *Andy's* way—he used hair-oil too!
'Why's a pretty girl like you working in a shop
like this?' he'd say, 'fancy a break? That's something
yours truly can readily provide.' Then, two years
later, 'Chris,' he wrote, 'I'm thinking of tying the knot—
and I kid you not (pun—or joke—intended)!'
But no follow-up came, unless you counted
that Christmas card saying 'Travel's my thing!'

And so it'd seem! Addis Ababa, Alexandria,
Aleppo, Damascus—what places, what charms
and life-styles lay behind those exotic names,
and Andy Gibson sampled them all, year
after year he sent bulletins; he was there
for work as well as fun, Overseas Sales now
in an expanding firm of ELT books.
Christopher felt his curiosity, rather than
his emotions, dimming. But how to respond?
'Must say, after you've been to some service in
an Eastern Christian church, you'll depart
pretty goddam happy, my old friend! A spot
of Kyrie eleison does all us guys a world of good!'

Exactly one month before Sally and he
and their two virtually grown-up kids moved
to their ecological rural Shropshire home,
'Hi there, Chris,' an email sang, 'you might have heard
that I made a right old rumpus in the famous
public gardens here,' but where was 'here' this time?
'Three days I strolled over lawns and past flower-beds
holding a cut-throat razor to my neck.
Was I going to use it on me? Probably not,
though who could be sure? I was still wanting,
poor fool, for all us alive to know how everything
that's light grows heavy, that what's transparent
turns dense, and that the world oppresses…. But
kind folk got worried, gave me ten days on Prozac
and a soothing bed-room, and guided me
into such changes as we all seek. So now I have song
and sympathy and age-old rites and thick
impregnable walls to keep me safe from
harm and evil, for ever, I do believe! Love from
your old(est?) friend, Andrew.'
                              'I'm glad to hear,'
wrote Christopher, 'you've found some safety…'
And from then on his email world had its
busiest member:
                              'How often, maybe several
times a day, I think of you and Sally (whom I
can recall with pleasure, you might say fondness),
leading a life that does the *world* good—just like,
I dare to hope, my own, as hostage to prayer.
Let me ask you about your new-found home—
whether your photovoltaic solar panels
bring not just electricity but happiness,
whether your condensing boilers which provide
under-floor heating also warm mind and heart?
Silly questions, but I ask them from a walled
seclusion where our one concern is for all
to be well.'

'I know that it is!' Christopher
hedged. But he always replies to Andy, for
might he not one day forsake those thick walls
of his, and for once simply take in what lies
all around him and feel awe at *that*? Besides,
deep inside him there's the distant April evening,
eleven o'clock striking, and a shower rustling
the boulevard chestnuts, and Andy turning to him
with 'What do you say to giving up on those French
whores, and being just two English blokes getting
together? EtceterA, etceterA, etceterA!'
Is that what happened, with foreign rain
on the windows of their cheap pension?
So much seems unclear now. Did old Gordon,
just before he died of cancer aged thirty-five,
really say: 'I don't mind my magnum opus
not being finished let alone published.
Nobody cares about "modern" any more!'?

'VAST SCRATCH-ARMIES'

Boys who turn their baseball caps
wrong way round defy the sun
to protect the backs of their necks.
Sweat-beads burst out on foreheads
as mementoes of duties
shelved, but peaks over napes
stave off the blows half-invited.
Vast scratch-armies, bemused by
the constant stir beneath denims,
shuffle our globe over—until
their involuntary dispersals
when sometimes redemption
nags, and starts at toes once dipped
into cold mountain freshets.

IN ARCHENFIELD

'Now, Howard, look to your left, as fine a view
of Archenfield as you'll get, its woods, its hills.
When we've crossed the little toll-bridge and paid
our sixpences (my duty to treat you your first time!),
you sh'd declare: "On Archenfield land/ Here I stand!"'
'Meaning…?' 'You're a local man, Howard Davies,
but you know next to nothing about the ancient
truths beneath your feet and before your eyes.
Heard of the Domesday Book? Well, Archenfield
gets mentioned there, caught between two countries.
Offa built his Dyke to keep the pesky Welsh out
but didn't bother with *here*, though Domesday
said it was England's whatever its folk felt.
They never gave up on their feelings. They were
Archenfielders, and that's all there was to it!
They were pretty like someone not a million
miles away, with a historic claim to being
an Archenfield Ergyng. When they'd to fight,
we Bowmen of Archenfield took no quarters….'

White-haired wizened old woman with a stick
operating from a tiny stone habitation
on the right-hand side of the bridge
over the Wye, fast and clear and full today,
she it is who takes our sixpences; I hate her
doing this: I can read her furrows, no need to
bother with her lips! 'Old Manor Farm's son's
paying for the Davies boy. His dad, you know,
is the auctioneer and estate-agent who's just
moved into *River Lea* out on the Hereford Road;
family's keen to get into the county set,
but they won't get as far as they want to….'
I don't think I'm keen to in the least, not unless
one member has a beautiful sister

with raven hair and a quiet husky voice,
and keen to get on with *her* I certainly am.

'We're going to climb The Knab now, Howard.
From there you can survey the Ergyngs' domain,
and as we go I'll outline the ideals
every true-souled Archenfielder should hold.'

I've won cups for long-runs and for sprinting
so if I am a bit breathless now, it's through
the force of Garth's words at me—who's never
more than inches behind him on this steep path—
words flying beyond, out and down, to the whole
ever-expanding West Herefordshire land:
the strings of black-and-white cottages, the
large riverside pub with garden and hop-field,
the acres of apple-orchards, the church on a knoll,
the cut hayfields spread out below the ridge
we're yet to scale, and the stump of a
small castle.
          'Castles cluster round these valleys
like bees round flowers. Sometimes I think, now
they're ivy-clad ruins, they're not human creations
so much as natural beings with feelings and wills
all their own. And they're on *my* side, Howard!'

Fair-haired (while I'm sandy!) with dark eyes (like
Ryllie's), Garth Whitwell seems now in tone and
stride the very master of this Knab we are climbing,
if not an Ergyng (all that's complete bollocks!).
The path has narrowed, the ferns on either side
have got taller and tougher, and yet don't block out
glimpses of wilder higher hills beyond this ridge.
'It's *wonderful* up here!' is what I want
to exclaim but something makes me say: 'Castles
don't have feelings, Garth, and even if they do,
other feelings would be more important still.'

'You're wrong there, Mr Davies, not for nothing
are you son of Mr *Maurice* Davies
of—we won't mention what firm. Its very name
might alarm the roe deer in these woods! If you turn
your Hereford suburban head round, you
can just make out my home, Old Manor Farm,
by that bend of the Wye shining bright in the
midday sun. You wouldn't want me, Howard,
to classify you with some of the Harbison
tribe who reject old beliefs for what's new and
nasty. Wouldn't you prefer to be bracketed
with someone at Old Manor who does truly
embrace them, my sister, Ryllie?....Oh yes,
I can see from your blushes—and don't put
them down to exertion, my friend—that you
would like to be bracketed with *her*, like
it a lot. But that's quite another matter
and has no place up here! Ergyng wisdom!'

Today I think—not for the first time—that
Garth was right and me wrong. These monuments
of the long-gone past which vegetation
has engulfed are animal and alive, whose
emotions, as well as looks, we should heed.
I know now what galled me into contradictory
mode was Garth paying for me at the toll-gate.
I wanted my own sixpence to pay me in.

I grew into quite a stickler for sixpences,
and still expect my counsellor's fees to be
paid as near on the dot as manageable
for qualified advice given after years
of social work. The kind of advice that
Ryllie and my son, Roland (but is he mine?)
dismiss. And sometimes, I confess, when
Ryllie in her lovely husky voice
describes the curious folk she's talked to

on Primrose Hill—or Roly, after a night's
clubbing, paints verbal pictures of louche
encounters—I can feel twinges of regret
that I didn't accept that Wye bridge toll-fee
willingly enough, that I followed Garth
with dissident feet, and reluctant ears,
quite sure I wasn't and couldn't be, an Ergyng.

REDSTREAKS

(an email)

Hi Andy, hope everything's fine with you.
Last night I dreamed I was back sitting in that
incongruous hall and clapping my hands off
at *Mail-man, Male-man,* and then the two of us
made off down a rainy boulevard, only
it wasn't Paris, merely a drab assortment
of one-level houses, shacks some of them,
can't think where! These last days Sally and I
have been doing a lot of travelling
but inside this region—we're true Marchers now!—
the hinterland of Clun, the Stretton hills
at their most challenging, and yesterday
in the opposite direction, thirty-five
miles from our home, Bredwardine on the Wye,
with the river in spate and the apple-trees
in blossom. And visited there an important
grave. You may think this an odd admission:
after all my years as a college teacher and
administrator concerned with literature,
there are only three writers I now can read:
Shakespeare, Wordsworth and—Francis Kilvert.
Don't suppose you've so much as heard of *him!*—
he wouldn't have been the old Andy Gibson's
cup of tea at all! He's been slumbering in
Bredwardine churchyard since 1879;
pilgrims come to his grave, and Sally and I
count ourselves among them. Actually I
left the hallowed spot before Sally, so
engrossed was she in her drawing of the place,
and walked alone to the Red Lion outside
which I had an encounter I want to tell you about.

He was sitting on the bench, oldish chap,
by which I mean he's roughly the same age
as you and me (we have to face *facts*, Andy!).
His sweater and trousers were not garments
you'd want to examine, the bulging tummy
hindering their hold, but at least he could
have given them—and himself—a good wash. He
realised my reaction. With as broad a smile
as I've ever seen, 'I'm all friendliness,'
he said, 'sit down and chat a while. Your
wife's still down by Kilvert's grave, isn't she?
I watched the two of you making your way there.
Stay till her return.' I really had no choice,
and wished to be kind. 'I'm Ivo Harbison.
Know my surname? That of one of the bigger
apple-families of this apple-rich country,
but they side-lined me early. You've just to
look at me to see I'm no businessman.'
(True!) 'Stephen and Johnno and Richard,
they're the *real* Harbisons they'd reckon.
But I can appreciate the finer points of
Redstreak, Herefordshire's Redstreak, far
better than they. It's an apple to be proud of:
from the 17th century, famous for years as
England's best for cider, then declining
and now reviving—the story all dream of.
It's bittersweet—and so are most of us,
me for instance, whose thoughts are often sad,
but whose sweetness of smile is sincere, wishing
most I talk to good fortune. Juicy Redstreaks
are small and round; all over the light yellow
run the always commanding streaks
of red, the colour of anger, passion, and
revolution. Wouldn't you say that *you*
(you haven't given me your name yet) are
something of a Redstreak, my new pal,
I feel quite sure you are.'

Just then we could see
Sally walking toward us and our conversation
(to call it that!!) had to end. But what old Ivo
said has reverberated, and I believe
him correct. No-one could be a better
judge of this than you, Andy, with fruit from
my past. Together we impressed old Gordon
e g about The Drama, together we lay
in that French pension, rain beating outside.
And, you know, I think you're a Redstreak too.

ENVOY

Just past the green ramparts of Clun Castle
the River Unk joins the River Clun.
Many people might not term either of them
'rivers', least of all the Unk. What a hard
scramble beneath those fortifications
looking down on this juncture entails!
The Clun, the bigger, is flowing eastward
after zigzag bends through well-farmed valley,
but thin Unk runs down from the north straight,
from the bare, lonely country of the Cefns (ridges).
'Clun' and 'Unk', more or less anagrams, both
believed pre-Celtic, the smaller evading all
identifiers. Obscure 'Unk' reminds us names
for vital waters are the oldest words we use.

I saw him over garden-wall of his fine
eco-house, tending his herb-bed and stroking
his grey cat. But I didn't call out to him
even though I'd crossed a continent and an
island-country with seeing him an objective.
Chris looked almost too serene in the soft
evening light. It wasn't that I didn't want to
meet him but that life—*I'm* getting on too!—
has taught me 'want' is never enough. 'Need'
is the better guide but the harder know.
Andy Gibson will still send Chris his emails,
but the realer him moves to this neighbourhood
after his sufficiency of flesh, cash and faiths.
From now he's like the Unk, arcane, confident.